The Everyday, the Mundane, and the Brave

poems by

Sarah Joy Nicole Thompson

Finishing Line Press
Georgetown, Kentucky

The Everyday, the Mundane, and the Brave

*This book is dedicated to the boys who plant seeds
of love in my heart every day and make trees grow:
my perpetually patient husband, Benjamin and our son, Viktor.*

Copyright © 2019 by Sarah Joy Nicole Thompson
ISBN 978-1-64662-047-0 First Edition
All rights reserved under International and Pan-American Copyright Conventions. No part of this book may be reproduced in any manner whatsoever without written permission from the publisher, except in the case of brief quotations embodied in critical articles and reviews.

ACKNOWLEDGMENTS

"About Waking Up" appeared in *100 Thousand Poets for Change San Antonio: Women SPEAK!*, 2018

Publisher: Leah Maines
Editor: Christen Kincaid
Cover Art: Sarah J. N. Thompson
Author Photo: Benjamin Thompson
Cover Design: Elizabeth Maines McCleavy

Printed in the USA on acid-free paper.
Order online: www.finishinglinepress.com
        also available on amazon.com

      Author inquiries and mail orders:
           Finishing Line Press
            P. O. Box 1626
        Georgetown, Kentucky 40324
               U. S. A.

Table of Contents

Only Kissing You Gets Better with Age 1
New Beat 2
Una Poema Oaxaqueña 3
Plazas de Oaxaca 4
June 20, 2016 Oaxaca 5
June 21, 2016 Oaxaca 6
A Lighthouse for The Youth 7
About Waking Up 8
Dear River 9
To My Sisters 10
Of Sisters 11
My Sister's Paintings 12
An Always Beautiful Mother 13
Ode to My Parents 14
The Feminine 15
My Thrift Store Guitar 16
Countdown Pie 17
Mornings in Our New Home 18
To the Morning 19
Spoken Verse 20
To Dance with You 21
Invest with Me 22
Noble Conclusion 23
20 Weeks Pregnant 24
On Breath and Birth 25
At First Sight 26
Mama's Milk Diary 27
Inhale; Exhale 28
Status Report: The Baby Is Crawling 29
To Your Restless Soul 30
My Hands Cannot Hold All of You 31
Little Feet 32
Earth and Heaven 33
Their Song 34

Only Kissing You Gets Better with Age

Kissing you at the end of the day
Reminds me of those times when we used to sit on the back porch
Of our first apartment
And jokingly discuss going on a vacation
To make a baby
I think the neighbors heard about
Our plans to go to Mexico and hike in the Sierra Norte
And stay in the cabin past the call for breakfast

It wasn't always legs wrapped around each other
And I'll never leave your side
I did leave, once
And you would write me often, to see if I was healing
After the pain of losing our vacation baby, our secret

I remember when I had the courage to see you again
So, I invited you to be my date at my sister's wedding
You saw me in the dark purple bridesmaid gown
And asked if we could walk by the beach before they cut the cake

Our hearts were still echoing some cries that were stifled
But we were learning how to speak
And out of the blue you said, "You have my heart,
And you can even eat it if you want"
I said don't make me cry
And you kissed me

New Beat

You and I are old news
we're weathered and sunburned
black and bruised
and we've come
to this point in our books
both dogged eared
and wondering why they forsook us
but we're writing new headliners
with our own first discoveries
like how beautiful sunsets are
when we're watching them over-eagerly
by a rooftop pool
the thrill of winning backgammon
three times in a row
laughing at your jokes
when we're standing in the checkout line
the art of crying under sunglasses
when we're pointing out silver linings in the sky

baby, we're making our come back
on this new road map of our lives
because somehow when you looked at me
you were the first responder
when I thought my heart couldn't beat

Una Poema Oaxaqueña

i. The weaver of dreams in this city
Comes often to visit me
She sits over my bed
She moves her hand gently
Moves it soft and slow
Telling a story in textiles
As I start to fall off the earth
And when she is near me
My feet don't touch the floor

ii. Her kisses are warm
And her kisses are sweet
They set sparks to the soul
Like a mug of hot atole
Her legs are strong from climbing
Pyramids all day
Her hands are rough from spinning
The clay of el barro de negro
Her hugs are comforting
Like the abuelita I never had
And her smile
Her smile es como el sol
Que se levanta sobre el mar

iii. Hay un pueblo
But it is starting to fade now
When I wake up the weaver is gone
Pero when she is near me
Es un baile en un sueño
Mis pies no tocan el suelo

Plazas de Oaxaca

I want to chip away at the stones
Where the folklore and cultural beliefs are stored
As webs of people
Go walking into the plaza
Pouring stories into these streets

They look right past me
Although I long to know
Their experiences, their memories
And the songs they sang
Before they hid their voices

I want to look into their eyes
And go the places they go
And touch the stones under their feet

June 20, 2016 Oaxaca

There is a girl who weaves
in and out of my dreams
I sleep light when she's threading
through my sleep
She blows on dandelions
and holds butterflies on her fingertips
She smiles up at me
and dances with no shoes on her feet
Sometimes she runs to me and says
let's make papa something sweet to eat
It's funny that she thinks about him
even though she rubs her tired eyes
and needs an afternoon nap

But her image fades
when there are real girls in Mexico
whose real mothers can't sleep at night
when I'm staring at a newspaper
that I can barely understand
And the headlines read
"La CNTE reporta once muertos por el enfrentamiento
en Nochixtlán, Oaxaca"
And the question remains
"Domingo sangriento en Oaxaca,
lo que sabemos y Lo que no"

June 21, 2016 Oaxaca

My host mom says
"Hoy está muy tranquilo en las calles
pero no salgan a el centro"
So I go about my day, and stay far away
From the Zocalo in Oaxaca City
Where los maestros para la union are encamped
With their makeshift tents and rain covers
They will march again tomorrow
Despite the threats to be forcibly removed by la policia

En la mañana classes are cancelled at la Mujica
The elementary school
Where the other UTSA students and I
Should be teaching English
Cancelled classes scare me the most
Because I am frightened
Frightened that the students
Are neglected in these protests
And no one is speaking for them
When they are too young to speak for themselves
And no matter what I do
The protests will continue

At night I lie down in a foreign bed, in a foreign country
Teary eyed I fabricate the little Spanish I know
¡Tengo miedo que la protesta vendrá!

A Lighthouse for The Youth

Is what a mother's love is
If I never have children
Who's to say I can't love
As mothers love
I will love the orphans
The ones that age out
Of the foster care systems
The ones bereft of a hideaway
A home base
The prodigal sons
Daughters
The boys who stow away on trains
The girls who sleep in older men's beds
The juveniles who are too young to wear jumpsuits
But were lured into the school to prison pipelines
And suffocated there
The teenage girls who hate themselves
And bleed babies from their hearts
Into the toilet
The ones who fall off the world
Jump off bridges
I will love them as if their real parents
Suddenly remembered how to
I will lead them home
I will kiss them
I will hold them
With my words
I will cry at their funerals

About Waking Up

Sometimes when I wake up in the morning
I feel like I am weighed down
By the paralysis of a broken-hearted day dream
Wherein I'm awake and moving mundanely through my day
And I'm reading about children
Separated from their mothers in the news
Robotically, unconsciously
All I do
Is donate small sums of money to various causes
Safely, from behind my key board
I donate $10 here, $20 there
Keeping my hands clean

But I can't do it any longer
I'm too tired of typing, clicking
Staying safe

The next time I wake up
I want to be enabled
To help those who can't walk
Can't reach, can't sing,
Can't even hold their mothers before they go to sleep
I'm tired of this day dream
I want to
Wake up

Dear River

Dear river, I have not yet written you a song
For I have not yet poured my tears into your waters
During the times of oppression, tyranny, and genocide
Like Jochebed who put her nursing babe into a basket
So he would not be drowned by the Pharaoh's decree
To kill the unwanted babies
For fear that they would overthrow the kingdom

And refugee mothers are no different than Jochebed
Who have swum alongside make shift rafts
To bring their babies to safer shores
Only to be turned away by gunmen waiting for their arrival

Dear river, if there should ever come a time
For me to give up my children for their own safety
Take all my possessions, my shattered dreams, my tears
But I beg you
To grant them safe crossing
And give them their kingdom

To My Sisters

I love you because

I would have my bones stretched
To give you the longer, stronger hug
You deserve in times of need

I would swim through choppy water
To help you stay afloat
In life's ever-changing seas

I would place you on a podium
And lace laurels around your neck
To show you your beauty within

I would lay down in the mud
If you had to step over my back
To get a little closer to heaven

Of Sisters

By my 24th trip
Around the sun
My sister's delicate arms
Could still envelope me
And make me feel
Like I had arrived
Somewhere important
If there was an idea of hope
My sister held it
In her hands
And painted it with watercolors
If I ever needed an encouraging word
It grew out of my sisters
Heart
And she nourished it
With love
If I ever felt desolate or lonely
I could look into my sister's eyes
And one look from her
Could tell me I was home

My Sister's Paintings

Our hearts are tin can telephones
dialing
when you're across the Pacific Ocean
you have a way to reach me
your paintings
are my falling asleep next to you stories
resonating from your heart
to your lotus fingertips
they kiss me good night
when your hair is too far away
to French braid
your hands are too far away
to hold
tonight, it's your brush
writing me these messages
across the string
singing me to sleep
good night, dear
Stephanie

An Always Beautiful Mother

My mother wore dresses
And lipstick, and her long black hair
And when she was done wearing those out
She put on her grey hair and her glasses
And some extra pounds
To hug me tight and hug me long
My mother is always in fashion
No matter what she wears

Ode to My Parents

The beauty is not in knowing
that you love me to this or that extent
the beauty is in this
that after I speak your names
I take a pause
to catch up with my breath
and while you are far away
I know I cannot alter time
or bend the geography of the earth
so I put my hand to my heart
in gratitude
knowing that a part of your hearts
is beating steadily in my chest

The Feminine

I put myself in other women's places
I am in grandmother, I am in mother
I am in daughter, I am in sister
I am in cousin, I am in friend
I am in the almost mother
I find myself in the sensitive
The emotional, the delicate

The unconditional love in me is found in other women
And their mothers have it too
If I love you it is because of your mother's love
My mother's love
Human nature
And my feminine instincts that made me
Give myself to you

My Thrift Store Guitar

Picking up Felicity after recuperating from a cold
And holding her sensually against my ribs
I get caught up on plucking each string
Feeling each word
Resonating in my lungs
Bouncing from my heart
To the roof of my mouth

And as I start to write my song
On the front porch
I sing about somewhere close to home
And never for a moment forget
The places that transcribed
The deep, sentient
Music of your soul

It's not about elevated lyrics
Or the technical side of a song
Sometimes it's just the intention

Countdown Pie

If I keep this up
I'll have to start making excuses
Did I say this was going to be a deep dish apple pie?
No it's a lean pie, obviously
I know the recipe only called for 3 pounds of apples
And we did get 4
But the apples shrunk in the pot
And the pie tin was bigger than I expected
So you'll just have to enjoy this
Quite shrunken, not so heaping,
Reduced filling apple pie
And I hope you like it the way it is
Because the roads are going to freeze tonight
And there's no point running back to the grocery store
So I'm sorry about this flat disc, more crust than apple kind of pie
But I hope you'll still kiss me at midnight
Happy New Year baby
From your loving wife,
Who couldn't stop eating the filling

Mornings in Our New Home

When you kiss me in the morning
the wind rattles through the window sills
to rouse our sleepy hearts,
a soft glow is born on my face
and we wake up before the clouds do
to press our tired skin together.
Methodically we wonder
what will grow from the green seeds
we stowed away in our youth,
the seeds that the wind carried out the window
and spilled into our front yard
and landed in the mulch.

I presume that when the rains
wash over San Antonio
to nurture the land
our roots will know which way to go.
Next to the brown brick
fresh stems will break the earth
and our branches
will grow so close together
the onlookers will travel to our home
to see if our roots are so intertwined
we have become one and the same tree.

To the Morning

Not too long from now
The night will wiggle away from me
And right before
I open my eyes
The earth will tingle
As you kiss me goodbye
Before your working day

And as I change my shirt
I will think of the way
You made my sleep sweet
For being in your arms
I find the sweetest sleep

Spoken Verse

If you never sought me
So that our hearts might rush and intertwine
I would feel like a hippy child.
I would sing the tune
Of one who feels forgotten, without a home
And my songs would sound
Like I was lost away in the wild.
Without your heart's home that is so welcoming to me
I am just a hippy on the beach
Looking for a family.
And I don't want to end up building
My own coffin in the sand
That I have been sitting in for days.

If you never had such love
To give me a fluently spoken verse,
I would lay down my living will
And be a hippy child.

But I know what sound I long to hear
When I travel home to you
It's the sound of your familiar voice
Your language spoken undefiled.

So as I come home to you
I just want to raise up my hands
And bow to the floor
And thank you for giving a home to this hippy child.

To Dance with You

In lieu of words
Dance is all the yearning
We wish to convey
From trembling, no, radiantly pulsing
Hearts
You take my hand in a confident grip
All too soon
My feet meet the air
My lungs are filled with angel breath
Your frenzied thoughts
Brush across my mind
We breathe words, touch words
Until we find the selves we need to express
We improvise
A coming of age story
Relived again and again.

Invest with Me

We invest in a savings account
For our dreams
Hoping someday to withdraw them
Spend them
At our leisure and ease
From time to time
I peek inside
To see barefoot strolls
On a white sand beach
With four-legged friends
And precious little feet
Piles of scrapbook memories
On a vintage table
With ring-like stains from our coffee and our tea
And imprints of family gatherings
Or a grandchild's crayon masterpiece

Our dreams, when plump, ripe, ready
Can be withdrawn and spent lavishly
And I'll relish each one
You withdraw beside me

Noble Conclusion

When the pigment of our hair has turned to white,
Our wrinkled feet turn less steadily,
Your smile will still bring me sheer delight,
In looking back on our moments shared
At life's grand table.

When our sight grows dull and hearing impaired,
You will be there to hold and assure me
"It was bliss with you all the while,
We have no need to say if only!"

20 Weeks Pregnant

Where are the words
that went down the drain
with my stomach acid
at 5 a.m. every morning
for the first twelve weeks
the words drowned
in NutriBullet® shakes
and oatmeal at 11 in the evening
the words I didn't keep
when I propped up my pillows
spread out my active birthing books
and fell asleep
the words that weren't spoken
while I was breathing my way
through pretend contractions
in prenatal yoga and kundalini

Somehow in my womb
you are catching for your mama
all the words I think are lost
on your fingertips, your heart
your breath when you breathe

Somehow I see
in you my son
books and books of poetry

On Breath and Birth

Sa. I look down at the boy wrapped snug against my chest
And say to him
Don't let me go alone
To and from the place that we know
To the place where we are waiting
Ta. There is a bright light overhead
My eyes are shut, dry from empty tear ducts
I am giving up, tired and exhausted
Everyone is yelling "He's almost here, he's almost here!"
I don't believe them
Until I reach down and feel the crown of a little head
Na. I take a deep breath
And push, straining the blood vessels in my eyes
Holding my legs apart, away from a quivering pelvis
Chin pressed to chest
Ma. And as if you and I are finally ready
You appear with a roaring cry
Animating every spirit in the room
Conveying a new zest to my soul
Some capable hands place you
Into my loving arms
And next to my heart
You feel
So at home
Sa. Ta. Na. Ma.

At First Sight

When you are ready, come into this world
and meet the woman with the heart that beat
next to your ears before you knew of sound
When you are ready, come into this world
and meet the woman who wrote
the lyrics to your creation before you knew of song
When you are ready, come into this world
and marvel with me for a long while
how it is possible to bestow a love so strong
on an unseen face
Because I, with all my heart, am ready
to meet the boy with the power
to turn a woman into a mother
an enduring pawn
into a queen

Mama's Milk Diary

Rosy lines like tiger stripes
are ripping the skin of my milk swollen breasts.
I stop looking in the mirror and try to change the subject
but keep thinking about milk—
the sweet, sticky, lingering presence of it
seems so omnipresent.
I'm starting to like the way it smells
on my shirts and sweaters
that I have to throw in the laundry
every single day.
Someone's beginning to cry for it now.
I best get to baby so he can ease
the sharp needle pricking sensation
that happens before let down.

And who knew a mother's milk
could be so messy?
Nursing pads are swamped
with the milk that should have been for baby
but is now leaking down the front of my body
onto the beltloops of my pants
onto baby's chubby legs.
I wipe it up with a burp cloth
and rub baby's dimply hands, baby's soft cheeks.
His silky skin makes up for the changes happening to mine
makes me forget about the rosy tiger stripes.

Inhale; Exhale

Time, you are a typo
you are repeated too frequently
you are omitted
too easily
you become a fragment
you become a run-on
stop
Time
you are a genius

Time, you are here
Time, you have played a trick on me
the minutes that I hold you
are uncountable

Status Report: The Baby Is Crawling

The upstairs banister is decorated
With a mason jar, a glass of water
Two dog bones, a chew toy giraffe
A half-eaten bowl of oatmeal
And an apple core
It has become the resting ground
For all things that the baby shouldn't play with

He started crawling on Wednesday
And I'm at the phase where I need personal space
More than ever

I can't stand it when he follows my footsteps
Into the bathroom and looks up at me
When I'm about to sit on the toilet
I'm also disappointed how rude it is
That he falls asleep while he's nursing
And the hopes of sneaking away without him waking up
Are fading

I should warn my husband now
Not to be alarmed if he comes home one day
And finds me sitting with my feet up
On the banister
Along with my emotions

To Your Restless Soul

When you would stir at night
with your clenched fists
I would whisper lullabies and untuck
your fingers
to put my palms in yours

We would fall
asleep again slowly
and I couldn't wait
to watch you dream
to watch you breathe

I slept light in those days
for how I loved
to wake up before you
to see the night had brought you peace
and look upon those sweet lips
and those sweet eyelashes

It was those daunting eyelashes
on the tips of your happy shut eyelids
that made me want to start my day

My Hands Cannot Hold All of You

You will have your four-month check up
On Thursday of this week
And as I watch you sleep
I have enlisted my heart
To hold the memory of you
Sleeping on the mattress on the floor
With the natural light from the window blinds
Pouring over your golden hair
Those thick eyelashes resting on your pale skin
A button like nose
And lips pursed into a cowboy hat

There are crickets calling the night to come
And I just watch and know
Although I cannot keep you by side
This way forever
You are in my heart
For always
To love and to hold

Little Feet

Amongst all the lights that come out at night
When the sun is gone
I see your light
So shine on
Little one
Amongst all the voices in the choir
The angels singing high and low
I recognize your voice
So sing on
Little one
Amongst the multitude of souls
Like grains of sand
That the waves pull into the sea
I know your soul
So live on
Little one

Earth and Heaven

Yours is the smile
That holds me in its grasp
That brings me a wave of comfort
That carries me to my dreams

Yours is the chest
Where I find the softest sleep

Yours is the face
That makes me a believer
That keeps me a pilgrim
That puts rhythm in my feet

Yours is the soul
Where the earth and heaven meet

Their Song

it was a song the island girls would sing
when they were lonely and gazing
out their windows at a pacific sky
on an island somewhere near the equator

it was a song they would sing
into karaoke machines at the top of their lungs
and while they were in the kitchen
cooking and scrubbing dishes

it was a song they would sing
the year they got breasts and menstrual cycles
and when they had their first babies
and learned that the road would be difficult
because they married for love and not for money

it was a song they would sing
when they learned that the budget was tight
and life wouldn't always treat them kind
because they wore the dress of poverty
but it didn't matter to them what they wore
if the little ones could at least eat one meal a day

it was a song they would sing
as they looked at their smiling babies
saying they would save every peso
for school tuition
so their children could have a chance

it was a song they would sing
when the cupboards were empty
and the little ones would sleep on the floor
crying for food late into the night

it was a song they would sing
during typhoons, and blown away roofs
and floods up to the chest
even in the face of death

they sang it knowing
they would soon lose their voices
and have no more air to carry the words

it was a song from the bottom of their big hearts
about the promises of a better life
a different future
not for them
but at least for their little ones
they sang and they sang
and they soon lost their voices

Sarah Thompson was born in the Philippines to an American father and Filipino mother. She spent her childhood and teenage years doing missionary work with her parents and siblings. Feeling the pressure to be constantly altruistic and self-sacrificing, she then participated in volunteer work and humanitarian programs with Rise Above Foundation Cebu, where she had her 18th birthday and began writing poetry.

Sarah's interest in writing impelled her to move to San Antonio to pursue a BA degree in English at the University of Texas at San Antonio. While in college, Sarah met fellow poets at open mic events hosted weekly by the Sun Poet's Society of San Antonio. Many poets in the group, along with the founder Rod Carlos Rodriguez, inspired her to continue writing and encouraged her to share her work with a larger audience. Sarah's poems have appeared in Sagebrush Review Volume XI, the Enigmatist, and 100 Thousand Poets for Change San Antonio: Women SPEAK!, 2018.

Seeing the world as a poem, Sarah continues to write about topics that readily surround her, including current happenings in the news, what she witnesses in her travels, and the immeasurable experiences that come with being a new mother. She has occasionally dedicated poems to her spouse, son, siblings, and parents, with whom she shares a strong bond.

Sarah is also an avid hiker, rock climber, photographer, and multidisciplinary artist. She resides in San Antonio, Texas with her husband, son, and a friendly family dog. In her free time, she finds joy in traveling, making music, writing songs, and creating art with her family.